MASTERING TH POCKET SQUARE A STEP-BY-STEP GUIDE

The Art of Pocket Square Mastery, A Comprehensive Guide to Elegant Folding Techniques

Sean Clement

OTHER BOOKS BY THIS AUTHOR

TABLE OF CONTENTS

3

INTRODUCTION

In the realm of men's fashion, accessories are the subtle yet powerful elements that transform an ordinary outfit into an extraordinary ensemble. Among these, the pocket square stands as a beacon of sartorial elegance, capable of adding a touch of sophistication, personality, and flair to any suit or blazer. This do-it-yourself book, "*Mastering the Art of Pocket Square Folding: A Step-by-Step Guide*," is your passport to the world of pocket square mastery, where the art of folding becomes a personalized expression of style.

Pocket squares have long been synonymous with refined dressing, serving as the pièce de résistance that completes a well-tailored look. These small, versatile pieces of fabric are not merely accessories; they are style statements that can subtly convey the wearer's personality, attention to detail, and a keen sense of fashion. Whether you're attending a formal gala, a business meeting, or a casual gathering, a thoughtfully folded pocket square has the power to distinguish you from the crowd, leaving a lasting impression of elegance and sophistication.

Within the pages of this guide, you will embark on a journey to master the art of pocket square folding, discovering a myriad of techniques that will elevate your style to new heights. Each fold is not just a mechanical process but a deliberate choice that complements the occasion, your outfit, and your personality. From the classic and timeless square fold to the intricate and regal Crown Fold, you will learn to wield the pocket square as a transformative tool, turning a simple garment into a canvas for self-expression. As you delve into the world of folds, you'll realize that pocket squares are more than just embellishments; they are a form of non-verbal communication. Each fold tells a story, reflects a mood, and conveys a message. Whether you opt for a Presidential Fold exuding authority or a whimsical Rose Fold expressing a romantic touch, your mastery of these folds will become a silent dialogue between you and the world, speaking volumes about your style sensibilities.

This book is not merely a set of instructions; it is an invitation to embark on a journey toward becoming a pocket square folding expert. With each turn of the page, you'll gain confidence in your ability to fold with precision and creativity. Anticipate the joy of experimenting with different folds, mixing and matching colors, and discovering the folds that resonate most with your personal style.

Whether you're a fashion enthusiast looking to enhance your wardrobe or a novice eager to explore the world of men's accessories, this guide is tailored to meet you where you are in your style journey. The anticipation lies in the moments of revelation and self-discovery as you navigate through the artful process of folding, draping, and presenting your pocket square with finesse.

So, dear reader, fasten your seatbelt and prepare for a captivating voyage into the realm of pocket square elegance. Your pocket square journey begins here, and by the end of this book, you will not only have mastered the folds but also discovered a newfound appreciation for the transformative power of this small yet mighty accessory.

"Style is knowing who you are, what you want to say, and not giving a damn." - Orson Welles

A LITTLE HISTORY

Origins Unveiled:

Now, picture a time when the pocket square was more than a fashion statement; it was a trusty sidekick with a job to do. Back in the day, our square companion wasn't just about looking dapper; it had a practical side hustle. Imagine a resourceful gent in Ancient Rome, using a small piece of cloth to wipe off the dust of the day—a proto-pocket square, if you will.

As we fast forward through the ages, we find these early pocket squares doubling as signals. In medieval Europe, a knight might tuck a small, embroidered piece into his pocket, signaling allegiance or marking a victorious joust. It was the original wearable art, telling tales of chivalry and triumph.

Historical Tapestry:

Now, let's stroll through history and catch snippets of conversations about pocket squares. In Renaissance Italy, the dashing courtiers didn't just wear pocket squares; they flaunted them with flair. It wasn't just about the fold; it was about the gesture—the nonchalant adjustment that spoke volumes.

Move forward a few centuries and witness the pocket square as a passport to exclusive literary salons. Picture Oscar Wilde, with a Wilde-ly flamboyant fold, holding court and making the pocket square an emblem of wit and sophistication.

From Function to Fashion:

And here we are, in the 20th century, where our pocket square takes a leisurely stroll from functionality to the epitome of fashion. The Jazz Age sees our square companion becoming a silent partner in the rhythm of the times. It wasn't just about wiping away specks of excess; it was about signaling a shift—a beat, if you will.

Casually draped into the pocket of a Hollywood leading man, the pocket square wasn't merely an accessory; it was a co-star, stealing scenes and adding that extra touch of suavity. Fast forward to today, and our pocket square continues to redefine casual elegance, seamlessly adapting to the changing tides of fashion.

"The joy of dressing is an art." - John Galliano

CHAPTER 1: ESSENTIAL TOOLS AND MATERIALS

Before diving into the intricacies of folding, it's imperative to familiarize yourself with the essential tools that will serve as the foundation for your pocket square journey. The primary protagonist, of course, is the pocket square itself. These small squares of fabric come in a variety of materials, patterns, and colors, each offering a unique opportunity for self-expression.

Equally crucial to your arsenal is an iron, your trusted companion in achieving crisp, polished folds. A well-ironed pocket square not only enhances the overall aesthetic but also showcases a meticulous attention to detail. Accompanying the iron, a flat surface provides the ideal workspace for perfecting your folds. A steady, smooth surface ensures precision and ease as you craft each fold with intention.

Elevating Your Look and Status with Pocket Squares

Pocket squares are not mere accessories; they are style catalysts that possess the power to transform an outfit from ordinary to extraordinary. In the realm of sartorial elegance, the pocket square emerges as a subtle yet impactful tool for self-expression. Its presence, neatly tucked into the pocket of a well-tailored jacket, serves as a testament to attention to detail and a discerning eye for style.

1. Distinctive Flair:

A carefully chosen pocket square introduces a touch of personality and flair, distinguishing you from the crowd. Whether it's a classic fold in silk or an unconventional material like leather or exotic skin, the pocket square is a canvas for showcasing your individuality.

2. Symbol of Sophistication:

Beyond being a mere accessory, the pocket square symbolizes sophistication and refined taste. It communicates an understanding of the nuances of fashion and an appreciation for the art of dressing well.

3. Elevates Formal Attire:

In formal settings, a pocket square elevates your attire to new heights. The choice of fold and material speaks volumes, adding an extra layer of elegance to suits and tuxedos, making you stand out in the most refined gatherings.

4. Status Symbol:

Historically, pocket squares were a mark of the aristocracy, and today, they continue to carry a certain status. When tastefully chosen and expertly folded, a pocket square communicates a sense of affluence and social standing.

5. Versatile Signifier:

The versatility of pocket squares allows them to be versatile signifiers, adapting to various occasions. Whether it's a casual fold in linen for a laid-back brunch or a silk pocket square for a formal event, it subtly communicates your understanding of appropriate style.

In essence, the pocket square is not just an accessory; it's a powerful tool that enhances your look and elevates your status. The artful selection and careful placement of this small square contribute to a narrative of sophistication, individuality, and an unwavering commitment to presenting oneself with style and panache.

Tips on Selecting the Right Fabric and Colors for Different Occasions

Selecting the appropriate fabric and color for your pocket square is an art that goes beyond mere coordination; it's a nuanced expression of style tailored to the specific occasion. Here are some tips to guide you in making thoughtful choices:

1. Formal Occasions:

- **Fabric:** Opt for luxurious and refined materials such as silk or fine cotton. Silk, with its smooth and lustrous texture, exudes an air of sophistication suitable for black-tie events or weddings. Crisp cotton can also be a viable option for a slightly more understated formal look.

- **Color:** Stick to classic and subdued tones like whites, creams, or solid pastels. These colors project a timeless elegance that complements the formality of the occasion.

2. Business and Professional Settings:

- **Fabric:** Choose pocket squares made from silk, wool, or a silk-wool blend for a polished yet versatile appearance.

These fabrics convey professionalism without being overly formal.

- **Color**: Opt for muted and conservative colors such as navy, burgundy, or subtle patterns. These choices strike a balance between professionalism and personal style.

3. Casual and Social Events:

- **Fabric**: Embrace the laid-back vibe with linen or cotton pocket squares. These fabrics bring a relaxed and breathable quality to your ensemble, perfect for social gatherings, outdoor events, or casual outings.

- **Color**: Feel free to experiment with bolder colors and patterns. Vivid blues, earthy tones, or playful prints can inject personality into your look, reflecting the casual nature of the event.

4. Seasonal Considerations:

- **Spring/Summer**: Lighter fabrics like linen or silk are ideal for warmer seasons. Embrace pastel shades and floral patterns to capture the vibrancy of spring and summer.

- **Fall/Winter**: Wool pocket squares provide warmth and texture during colder months. Earthy tones, deep greens, and rich burgundies complement the seasonal atmosphere.

5. Bold and Creative Statements:

- **Fabric**: Experiment with unique textures like knits or blends for a distinctive touch. Velvet or patterned silk can add an unexpected twist to your ensemble.

- **Color**: Feel free to express your creativity with vibrant colors, intricate patterns, or even themed designs. This is your opportunity to showcase your personality and make a bold fashion statement.

6. Matching with Your Outfit:

- **Complementary Colors**: Choose a pocket square that complements the colors of your tie, shirt, or suit. Harmonizing tones create a cohesive and well-thought-out look.

- **Contrast for Impact**: Alternatively, opt for a pocket square that contrasts with your outfit to add visual interest. A pop of color or a distinct pattern can be a conversation starter.

Remember, the key is to strike a balance between personal style and appropriateness for the occasion. Your pocket square is not just an accessory; it's a tool for self-expression that enhances your overall look. By carefully considering fabric and color choices, you'll master the art of selecting the perfect pocket square for any event.

Care Instructions for Maintaining the Longevity of Pocket Squares

Taking proper care of your pocket squares is essential to ensure they remain vibrant, crisp, and ready to elevate your style for years to come. Follow these care instructions to preserve the longevity of your pocket squares:

1. Cleaning Methods:

-Dry Cleaning for Delicate Fabrics: For silk or other delicate fabrics, consider professional dry cleaning. This method ensures a thorough clean without risking damage to the material. Be sure to communicate any specific concerns or stains to the dry cleaner for tailored care.

- Gentle Handwashing for Cotton and Linen: For cotton or linen pocket squares, gentle handwashing is often suitable. Use mild detergent and cold water, and avoid wringing the fabric, as this can distort its shape. Allow the pocket square to air dry.

2. Storage Practices:

- Flat Storage: Store your pocket squares flat to maintain their shape. If possible, keep them in their original packaging or in a dedicated pocket square organizer. Avoid overcrowding to prevent unnecessary creasing.

- Protective Barriers: Consider placing a barrier, such as tissue paper or a fabric pouch, between folded pocket squares to prevent friction and potential damage.

3. Ironing Guidelines:

- Temperature Settings: Adjust the iron temperature based on the fabric of the pocket square. Low to medium heat is suitable for delicate fabrics like silk, while higher temperatures can be used for cotton and linen. Always test a small, inconspicuous area first.

- Use a Pressing Cloth: Place a pressing cloth, such as a clean cotton fabric, between the iron and the pocket square to protect the material from direct heat. This is especially crucial for silk and other sensitive fabrics.

4. Rotation of Use:

- Even Distribution: Rotate your pocket squares regularly to ensure even wear. This prevents one or a few pocket squares from becoming overused, extending the overall lifespan of your collection.

5. Inspection and Spot Cleaning:

- Routine Checkups: Periodically inspect your pocket squares for any signs of damage, loose threads, or stains. Addressing issues promptly can prevent further deterioration.

- Spot Cleaning: If you notice a stain, attend to it immediately using a targeted spot-cleaning method. Blot the stain gently with a clean cloth or sponge, and avoid rubbing, which can worsen the stain.

6. Avoiding Harsh Chemicals:

- Be Mindful of Products: Avoid exposure to harsh chemicals, such as perfumes, colognes, or hairsprays, which can damage the fabric over time. Apply grooming products before donning your pocket square to minimize contact.

7. Environment Considerations:

- Protect from Sunlight: Prolonged exposure to direct sunlight can fade colors over time. Store your pocket squares in a cool, dark place to minimize sun damage.

By incorporating these care instructions into your routine, you'll not only extend the life of your pocket squares but also ensure they continue to enhance your style with every wear. Treating each pocket square with care and attention will preserve their beauty and make them enduring staples in your wardrobe.

"To me, clothing is a form of self-expression – there are hints about who you are in what you wear." - Marc Jacobs

CHAPTER 2: BASIC FOLDING TECHNIQUES

In this chapter, we delve into the foundational art of folding, where simplicity meets elegance. These basic folding techniques are the building blocks of pocket square mastery, each fold presenting a unique character and mood. Whether you're aiming for a classic and timeless appearance or a more relaxed and casual vibe, mastering these folds will set the stage for your pocket square journey.

1. Classic Fold

The classic fold is the epitome of timeless elegance, a simple yet refined way to adorn your suit or blazer pocket.

Step-by-Step Instructions:

- Lay the pocket square flat on a clean, smooth surface.

- Fold the square in half to form a rectangle.

- Fold it in half again, creating a smaller square.

- Adjust the size as needed, ensuring it fits snugly within your pocket.

- Insert the folded square into your pocket, leaving just enough to showcase the top edge.

Styling Tip: The classic fold is versatile and suits formal occasions seamlessly. It complements a wide range of suits and shirts, making it a reliable choice for a polished and sophisticated look.

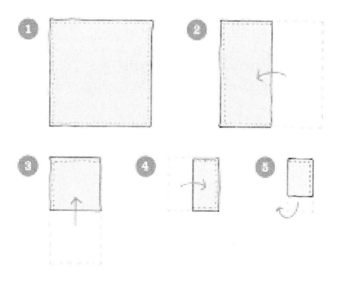

2. One-Point Fold

The one-point fold adds a subtle touch of sophistication with a single pointed tip peeking out from your pocket.

Step-by-Step Instructions:

- Begin with the pocket square laid flat.

- Fold it diagonally to create a triangle.

- Fold one corner toward the center.

- Repeat with the opposite corner, forming a shape resembling an envelope.

- Adjust the size to fit your pocket, ensuring the single point is visible when inserted.

Styling Tip: This fold is perfect for occasions where you want to convey a refined and understated elegance. It pairs well with business attire and formal events, adding a subtle focal point.

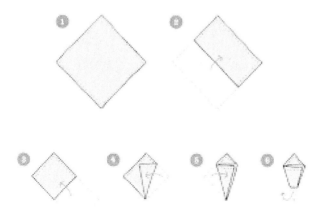

3. Two-Point Fold

Elevate your style with the two-point fold, a slightly more intricate technique that exudes flair and sophistication.

Step-by-Step Instructions:

- Start with the pocket square laid flat.

- Fold it diagonally to form a triangle.

- Fold one corner towards the center, creating a smaller triangle.

- Repeat with the opposite corner, forming a shape resembling a three-layered pyramid.

- Adjust the size as needed before inserting it into your pocket.

Styling Tip: The two-point fold is an excellent choice when you want to add a touch of individuality to your ensemble. It works well for both formal and semi-formal events, making a subtle statement.

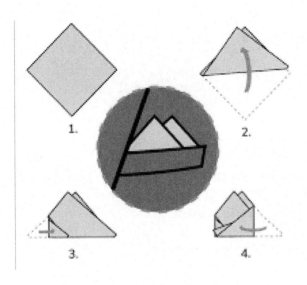

4. The Puff Fold

Embrace a more relaxed and casual vibe with the puff fold, a free-spirited and effortless way to wear a pocket square.

Step-by-Step Instructions:

- Hold the pocket square from the center.

- Gently gather the fabric, allowing it to naturally puff.

- Adjust the size and shape of the puff as desired.

- Insert the gathered end into your pocket, allowing the puff to rest on top.

Styling Tip: The puff fold is perfect for informal events, adding a touch of nonchalance to your look. It pairs well with casual blazers and creates an approachable and laid-back appearance.

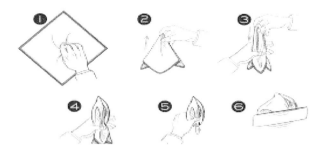

5. The Diagonal Fold

The diagonal fold adds a dynamic and diagonal flair to your pocket square, injecting a sense of movement and energy into your ensemble.

Step-by-Step Instructions:

- Begin with the pocket square laid flat.

- Fold it diagonally to create a triangle.

- Fold the bottom corner of the triangle towards the top corner, creating a smaller triangle with a diagonal edge.

- Adjust the size and tightness of the fold to fit your pocket.

- Insert the folded square with the diagonal edge prominently displayed.

Styling Tip: The diagonal fold is an excellent choice for those seeking a slightly unconventional yet still polished look. It adds a modern touch to your outfit and can be adapted for both formal and semi-formal occasions.

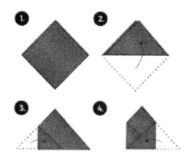

6. The Reverse Puff Fold

A variation of the classic puff, the reverse puff fold creates a unique and eye-catching puff effect, turning heads with its distinctive appearance.

Step-by-Step Instructions:

- Hold the pocket square from the center, just like with the classic puff.

- Instead of gathering the fabric towards the center, twist the fabric in the opposite direction, creating a reverse puff effect.

- Adjust the size and shape of the reverse puff to your liking.

- Insert the twisted end into your pocket, allowing the reverse puff to rest on top.

Styling Tip: The reverse puff fold is a playful and stylish choice, ideal for casual and social settings where you want to showcase a touch of personality. It works well with a variety of pocket square sizes and can be particularly effective with patterned or textured fabrics.

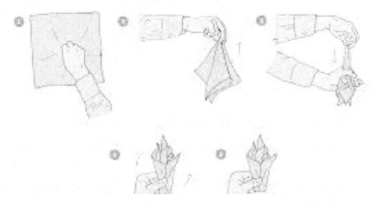

By mastering these basic folding techniques, you're laying the foundation for a diverse and expressive pocket square repertoire. These folds are not just about presentation; they're about conveying your style narrative with every carefully crafted pocket square arrangement. As you experiment with these techniques, you'll discover the subtle art of folding as a means of self-expression and style distinction.

"Fashion is about dressing according to what's fashionable. Style is more about being yourself." - Oscar de la Renta

CHAPTER 3: INTERMEDIATE FOLDS

In this chapter, we explore intermediate folds that take your pocket square game to the next level. These folds offer a balance between sophistication and creativity, making them perfect for a range of occasions. Let's dive into the art of folding that transcends the basics.

1. The Presidential Fold

The Presidential Fold is the epitome of crisp elegance, making it an ideal choice for formal and business events.

Step-by-Step Instructions:

- Start with the pocket square laid flat.

- Fold it into quarters, creating a smaller square.

- Adjust the size to fit your pocket.

- Insert the folded square, showcasing a neat and precise square edge.

Styling Tip: The Presidential Fold is a power move, conveying authority and attention to detail. It pairs exceptionally well with tailored suits and is perfect for occasions where a distinguished and commanding appearance is desired.

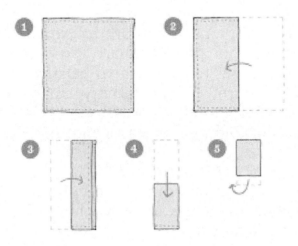

2. The Winged Puff

Elevate the classic puff with a touch of flair by adding wing-like edges, striking the perfect balance between sophistication and playfulness.

Step-by-Step Instructions:

- Begin with the pocket square laid flat.

- Create a classic puff fold as described earlier.

- Pinch and fold the sides of the puff, creating wing-like edges.

- Adjust the size and shape to achieve a harmonious balance between the puff and wings.

- Insert the folded square, ensuring the wings are visible.

Styling Tip: The Winged Puff adds a stylish twist to the classic puff, making it suitable for events where you want to showcase a creative and distinctive touch. It works well with both solid and patterned pocket squares.

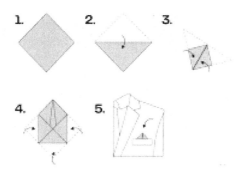

3. The Scallop Fold

The Scallop Fold introduces a series of small, rounded peaks along the top edge of the pocket square, creating a visually interesting and textured appearance.

Step-by-Step Instructions:

- Lay the pocket square flat.

- Fold it in half to create a rectangle.

- Fold the bottom edge upwards, creating a small cuff.

- Repeat the folding process, creating multiple small cuffs along the bottom edge.

- Adjust the size and spacing of the cuffs to achieve a scalloped effect.

Styling Tip: The Scallop Fold adds a touch of whimsy and sophistication, making it an excellent choice for events where you want to showcase a unique and intricate fold. It works particularly well with silk or patterned pocket squares.

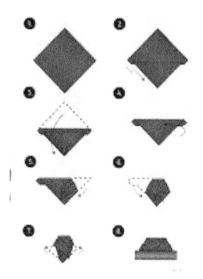

4. The Stair-Step Fold

The Stair-Step Fold creates a distinctive tiered effect, resembling a set of cascading steps. It's a fold that stands out with its structured and eye-catching appearance.

Step-by-Step Instructions:

- Begin with the pocket square laid flat.

- Fold it in half diagonally to create a triangle.

- Fold the bottom corner of the triangle upwards, creating a smaller triangle with a straight base.

- Repeat the folding process, creating multiple triangles stacked on top of each other.

- Adjust the size and spacing of the steps to achieve the desired effect.

Styling Tip: The Stair-Step Fold is a statement fold, perfect for events where you want to make a bold impression. It works well with solid-colored pocket squares and can add a touch of drama to your overall look.

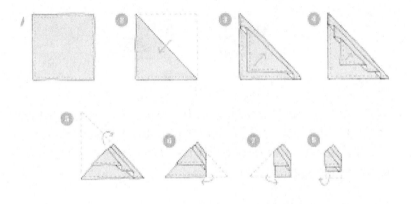

5. The Crown Fold

The Crown Fold is a regal and intricate fold resembling a crown, making a bold and majestic statement.

Step-by-Step Instructions:

- Start with the pocket square laid flat.

- Create a series of accordion-like folds along one edge, forming peaks and valleys.

- Fold the square in half, securing the accordion folds in place.

- Adjust the size and shape of the crown by fluffing the peaks.

Styling Tip: The Crown Fold is a distinctive choice for special occasions, adding an air of grandeur to your ensemble. It pairs well with solid-colored pocket squares and can be a conversation starter at formal events.

These intermediate folds provide an opportunity to showcase your creativity and individuality. Experiment with different fabrics, patterns, and sizes to discover the folds that resonate most with your personal style. As you master these folds, you'll find that pocket squares become not just accessories but expressions of your unique sartorial identity.

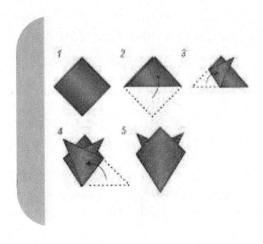

"Elegance is not standing out but being remembered." - Giorgio Armani

CHAPTER 4: ADVANCED FOLDS

In this chapter, we explore advanced folds that elevate pocket square folding to an art form. These folds are intricate, sophisticated, and add a touch of complexity to your ensemble, making a statement that goes beyond the ordinary.

1. The Rose Fold

The Rose Fold transforms your pocket square into a delicate and intricate rose, creating a focal point that exudes romance and sophistication.

Step-by-Step Instructions:

- Begin with the pocket square laid flat.

- Fold the square into a triangle.

- Start folding the base of the triangle, creating tight and consistent folds.

- Roll the folded base to form the center of the rose.

- Adjust the outer layers to create the petals, shaping the rose to your liking.

Styling Tip: The Rose Fold is perfect for special occasions where you want to make a romantic or refined statement. It works well with silk or satin pocket squares and pairs beautifully with formal attire.

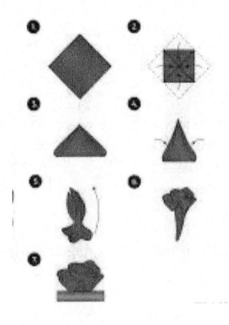

2. The Cascade Fold

The Cascade Fold introduces a cascading effect, resembling a waterfall of fabric, creating a sophisticated and eye-catching appearance.

Step-by-Step Instructions:

- Begin with the pocket square laid flat.

- Fold the square into a triangle.

- Start folding the base of the triangle in small, even folds.

- Continue folding until you reach the tip of the triangle, creating a cascade of layered folds.

- Adjust the size and spacing of the folds to achieve the desired cascading effect.

Styling Tip: The Cascade Fold is a dramatic choice, adding flair to your ensemble. It works well with solid-colored or patterned pocket squares and is particularly suited for formal events where you want to make a bold yet elegant impression.

"Fashion is like eating, you shouldn't stick to the same menu." - Kenzo Takada

3. The Shell Fold

The Shell Fold creates a unique and sculptural appearance reminiscent of a seashell, adding an element of intrigue to your pocket square presentation.

Step-by-Step Instructions:

- Begin with the pocket square laid flat.

- Fold the square into a triangle.

- Fold the base of the triangle upward, creating a straight line.

- Fold the sides of the triangle inwards, forming a rectangle with a pointed top.

- Fan out the layers, adjusting the size and shape to resemble a shell.

Styling Tip: The Shell Fold is a conversation starter, perfect for events where you want to showcase your creativity. It pairs well with textured or patterned pocket squares and adds a touch of whimsy to your look.

4. The Spiral Fold

The Spiral Fold creates a visually dynamic and captivating effect, resembling a spiraled vortex of fabric that draws attention.

Step-by-Step Instructions:

- Begin with the pocket square laid flat.

- Fold the square into a triangle.

- Start folding the base of the triangle in a continuous spiral pattern.

- Continue folding until you reach the tip of the triangle, forming a tight and visually striking spiral.

- Adjust the size and spacing of the folds to achieve the desired spiral effect.

Styling Tip: The Spiral Fold is a bold choice that adds a modern and artistic touch to your ensemble. It works well with solid-colored pocket squares, allowing the intricate spiral to take center stage.

5. The Fan Fold

The Fan Fold creates a dramatic and structured appearance, resembling a fan that unfolds in a symmetrical pattern.

Step-by-Step Instructions:

- Begin with the pocket square laid flat.

- Start folding the pocket square accordion-style in even sections.

- Fold the accordion in half, creating a fan-like structure.

- Adjust the size and spacing of the folds to achieve a balanced and symmetrical fan shape.

- Insert the folded square into your pocket, allowing the fan to open slightly.

Styling Tip: The Fan Fold is a statement-making choice, perfect for events where you want to showcase your bold and confident style. It pairs well with solid-colored or subtly patterned pocket squares and adds a touch of theatricality to your look.

As you explore these advanced folds, remember that practice is key to achieving mastery. Experiment with different fabrics, colors, and sizes to discover the folds that resonate most with your personal style. These advanced folds are not just about folding fabric; they are about creating wearable art that reflects your unique sartorial identity.

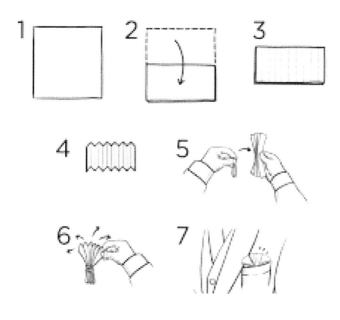

Style is a way to say who you are without having to speak." - Rachel Zoe

CHAPTER 5: SEASONAL AND THEME-BASED FOLDS

In this chapter, we explore the versatility of pocket square folding by delving into seasonal and theme-based folds. Whether you're celebrating a festive holiday, attending a wedding, or aiming for a casual and playful look, these folds add a thematic touch to your ensemble, making your pocket square a dynamic accessory that adapts to various occasions.

1. Holiday Folds

Holiday folds are designed to capture the spirit of festive occasions, adding a touch of celebration to your attire.

The Christmas Tree Fold

Step-by-Step Instructions:

- Begin with the pocket square laid flat.

- Fold the square into a triangle.

- Start folding the base of the triangle upward, creating a series of tight folds.

- Adjust the size and shape to resemble a Christmas tree.

- Add a small star-shaped lapel pin or a gold-colored fold at the top for decoration.

Styling Tip: The Christmas Tree Fold is perfect for holiday parties and gatherings. Pair it with festive colors like red, green, or gold to complete the seasonal look.

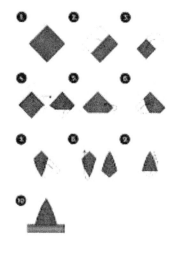

The Festive Bow Fold

Step-by-Step Instructions:

- Begin with the pocket square laid flat.

- Fold the square into a rectangle.

- Create a series of accordion folds along the center of the rectangle.

- Secure the folds at the center with a decorative pin, creating a bow-like appearance.

- Adjust the size and spacing of the folds for a festive bow effect.

Styling Tip: The Festive Bow Fold adds a playful and celebratory touch, making it suitable for holiday parties and formal events. Choose colors that complement your outfit and the festive theme.

2. Wedding Folds

Wedding folds are elegant and refined, tailored for grooms and wedding attendees seeking a sophisticated touch.

The Wedding Cake Fold

Step-by-Step Instructions:

- Begin with the pocket square laid flat.

- Fold the square into a rectangle.

- Create a series of accordion folds along the center of the rectangle.

- Gradually fan out the folds, creating a tiered effect resembling a wedding cake.

- Adjust the size and spacing of the folds for a balanced and elegant appearance.

Styling Tip: The Wedding Cake Fold is a graceful choice for weddings, adding a touch of sophistication to your formal attire. Opt for classic colors like white or cream to complement the wedding theme.

The Tuxedo Fold

Step-by-Step Instructions:

- Begin with the pocket square laid flat.

- Fold the square into a rectangle.

- Fold one corner diagonally to create a triangle.

- Fold the two side corners of the triangle towards the center.

- Adjust the size and positioning to resemble the lapels of a tuxedo.

Styling Tip: The Tuxedo Fold is a classic and timeless choice, perfect for formal weddings. Coordinate the color of the pocket square with the wedding color scheme for a cohesive look.

3. Casual and Fun Folds

Casual and fun folds are playful, creative, and perfect for more relaxed events.

The Paper Airplane Fold

Step-by-Step Instructions:

- Begin with the pocket square laid flat.

- Fold the square into a rectangle.

- Fold the two side corners diagonally towards the center.

- Fold the top edges downward, creating a triangular shape resembling a paper airplane.

- Adjust the size and shape for a whimsical touch.

Styling Tip: The Paper Airplane Fold is lighthearted and ideal for casual gatherings or outdoor events. Choose vibrant and playful colors to enhance the fun theme.

The Pocket Fan Fold

Step-by-Step Instructions:

- Begin with the pocket square laid flat.

- Fold the square into a rectangle.

- Create a series of accordion folds along the center of the rectangle.

- Secure the folds at the center, creating a fan-like appearance.

- Adjust the size and spacing of the folds for a playful pocket fan.

Styling Tip: The Pocket Fan Fold is a quirky and creative choice for casual events. Experiment with patterned or boldly colored pocket squares to showcase your personality.

These seasonal and theme-based folds allow you to tailor your pocket square to the occasion, adding a thematic and personalized touch to your ensemble. As you explore these folds, feel free to experiment with colors, patterns, and accessories to fully embrace the spirit of the season or theme.

CHAPTER 6: TROUBLESHOOTING AND TIPS

In this chapter, we address common pitfalls and offer valuable tips to enhance your pocket square folding expertise. Mastering the art involves not only knowing how to fold but also understanding how to troubleshoot issues and make informed choices based on various factors.

Common Mistakes and How to Avoid Them

Overcomplicated Folds

- Issue: Attempting overly intricate folds without sufficient practice can result in a messy or unpolished appearance.

- Solution: Start with basic folds and gradually progress to more complex ones as your proficiency improves. Practice regularly to achieve precision.

Poor Fabric Choice

- Issue: Choosing the wrong fabric for the occasion or season can impact the overall aesthetic.

- Solution: Understand the characteristics of different fabrics and select accordingly. Opt for breathable fabrics like linen for summer and luxurious options like silk for formal events.

Misjudging Size

- Issue: A pocket square that's too large or too small can disrupt the balance of your outfit.

- Solution: Adjust the size based on your pocket dimensions. Ensure the pocket square doesn't overwhelm the pocket but is visible enough to make an impact.

Inconsistent Folding

- Issue: Each fold appearing different can create a lack of cohesion in your overall look.

- Solution: Maintain consistency in your folding technique. Practice achieving uniformity in size, shape, and positioning.

Tips for Matching Pocket Squares with Different Suits and Shirts

Color Coordination

- Tip: Choose pocket squares that complement the dominant colors in your outfit. Harmonize with the shirt, tie, or suit for a cohesive look.

Pattern Play

- Tip: Mix patterns thoughtfully. If your shirt or tie has a bold pattern, opt for a more subtle pattern or solid color pocket square to avoid visual overload.

Fabric Harmony

- Tip: Match the formality of the fabric with the occasion. Silk for formal events, linen for casual gatherings. Ensure the fabric weight complements the rest of your outfit.

Contrast for Impact

- Tip: Experiment with contrasting colors to add interest. A well-chosen contrasting pocket square can be a striking focal point.

e. Occasion Appropriateness

- Tip: Tailor your choice based on the event. Formal occasions may call for classic folds and subdued colors, while casual settings allow for more creativity and vibrancy.

Adjusting Folds Based on Pocket Square Size and Fabric Type

Small Pocket Squares

- Tip: Opt for simpler folds with small pocket squares to avoid overcrowding. Classic folds like the puff or one-point fold work well.

Large Pocket Squares

- Tip: Larger squares allow for more intricate folds. Experiment with advanced folds like the rose or cascade for a dramatic effect.

Delicate Fabrics

- Tip: Handle delicate fabrics like silk with care. Use a pressing cloth when ironing and store them flat to maintain their sheen and texture.

d. Sturdy Fabrics

- Tip: Robust fabrics like cotton or wool can hold complex folds well. Experiment with more structured folds for added flair.

Experimentation

- Tip: Don't be afraid to experiment. Try different folds, fabrics, and combinations to discover what suits your style and the occasion best.

Formality Factor

- Tip: Reserve intricate folds like the rose or cascading folds for formal events. Simple folds like the classic or one-point are suitable for everyday wear.

Remember, the key is practice and a willingness to experiment, allowing you to refine your skills and develop a nuanced understanding of the art of pocket square folding.

"*Fashion is the armor to survive the reality of everyday life.*" - Bill Cunningham

CONCLUSION

As we conclude this journey through the artistry of pocket square folding, let's reflect on the key techniques that have adorned our sartorial voyage. From the timeless elegance of the Classic Fold to the sophisticated allure of the Cascade Fold, we've explored a myriad of styles that transform a simple piece of fabric into a statement of personal expression.

In this tapestry of folding techniques, each method carries its own narrative—a story woven into the fabric of your attire. The Presidential Fold commands attention with its authoritative precision, while the whimsical Paper Airplane Fold adds a touch of playfulness to your ensemble. Whether you're donning a Tuxedo Fold for a grand event or a relaxed Puff Fold for a casual gathering, each fold is a brushstroke, painting the canvas of your style.

As you embark on your pocket square folding endeavors, I encourage you to be not just a follower of these techniques but a composer of your own symphony. The true beauty lies in the experimentation, the moments of inspiration when you discover folds that resonate with your unique essence. Just as every fold tells a story, every choice you make is a brushstroke, shaping the masterpiece that is your personal style.

Remember, style is not bound by rules but defined by individuality. Dare to experiment, to push the boundaries, and to celebrate the fluidity of fashion. Your pocket square is not merely an accessory; it is a canvas waiting for your creative expression. Let it reflect the colors of your personality, the patterns of your passions, and the folds of your journey.

I extend my deepest gratitude to you, dear reader, for embarking on this folding adventure. It has been an honor to guide you through the intricacies of pocket square artistry. Your journey does not end here; it continues with each fold you create each style you embrace, and each occasion you grace with your unique touch.

As you embark on your own pocket square odyssey, I invite you to share your experiences. Your stories, your triumphs, and even the folds that challenged you—we want to hear them all. Let us build a community bound by the love of style and the joy of pocket square folding.

May your folds be ever elegant, your styles ever evolving, and your pocket squares forever a canvas of self-expression. Until we meet again in the world of tailored elegance, happy folding!

APPENDIX

In the spirit of practicality and quick reference, this appendix serves as your go-to pocket square folding cheat sheet. Whether you're getting ready for a formal event, a casual gathering, or simply seeking a touch of sartorial flair, this guide will be your trusted companion. Below, you'll find a concise summary of key folding techniques to suit various occasions.

1. Classic Fold

- Fold the pocket square into a rectangle and then into a smaller square.

- Insert into the pocket, leaving the top edge visible.

2. One-Point Fold

- Fold the pocket square into a triangle.

- Fold one corner toward the center, creating a single pointed tip.

- Adjust and insert into the pocket.

3. Two-Point Fold

- Fold the pocket square into a triangle.

- Fold both corners toward the center, forming two distinct points.

- Adjust and insert into the pocket.

4. Puff Fold

- Gently gather the pocket square from the center.

- Adjust the size and puffiness.

- Insert the gathered end into the pocket, allowing the puff to rest on top.

5. Diagonal Fold

- Fold the pocket square into a triangle.

- Fold the bottom corner toward the top corner, creating a diagonal edge.

- Insert into the pocket with the diagonal edge visible.

6. Reverse Puff Fold

- Hold the pocket square from the center.

- Twist the fabric in the opposite direction, creating a reverse puff.

- Adjust and insert into the pocket.

7. The Rose Fold

- Fold the pocket square into a triangle.

- Fold the base in tight, consistent folds.

- Roll the folded base to form the center of the rose.

- Shape the outer layers into petals.

8. The Cascade Fold

- Fold the pocket square into a triangle.

- Begin folding the base in small, even folds.

- Continue folding, creating a cascading effect.

- Adjust and insert into the pocket.

9. The Fan Fold

- Fold the pocket square accordion-style in even sections.

- Fold in half, creating a fan-like structure.

- Adjust and insert into the pocket, allowing the fan to open slightly.

10. The Shell Fold

- Fold the pocket square into a triangle.

- Fold the base upward, creating a straight line.

- Fold the sides inward, forming a rectangle with a pointed top.

- Fan out the layers to resemble a shell.

This cheat sheet is designed for quick and easy access, providing a visual reminder of the steps involved in each folding technique. Keep this guide handy in your wardrobe or dresser for those moments when you want to add a touch of sophistication to your ensemble. Happy folding!

"Fashion you can buy, but style you possess. The key to style is learning who you are, which takes years. There's no how-to road map to style. It's about self-expression and, above all, attitude." - Iris Apfel

61